DATE DUE

SEP 20 2014	
JUN 05 2015	
AUG 10 2016	

MANNERS MATTER
ON THE
PLAYGROUND

BY LORI MORTENSEN

ILLUSTRATED BY LISA HUNT

CAPSTONE PRESS
a capstone imprint

First Graphics are published by Capstone Press,
151 Good Counsel Drive, P.O. Box 669, Mankato, Minnesota 56002.
www.capstonepub.com

Books published by Capstone Press are manufactured with paper
containing at least 10 percent post-consumer waste.

Library of Congress Cataloging-in-Publication Data
Mortensen, Lori, 1955–
  Manners matter on the playground / by Lori Mortensen ; illustrated by Lisa Hunt.
    p. cm. — (First graphics manners matter)
  Includes bibliographical references.
  ISBN 978-1-4296-5332-9 (library binding)
  ISBN 978-1-4296-6226-0 (paperback)
  1. Student etiquette—Comic books, strips, etc. 2. Playgrounds—Comic books, strips,
etc. 3. Recesses—Comic books, strips, etc. I. Hunt, Lisa (Lisa Jane), 1973– II. Title.
III. Series.

  BJ1857.S75M37 2011
  395.5—dc22

                                    2010028923

Editor: **Shelly Lyons**
Designer: **Juliette Peters**
Art Director: **Nathan Gassman**
Production Specialist: **Eric Manske**

Printed in the United States of America in Stevens Point, Wisconsin.
092010   005934WZS11

TABLE OF CONTENTS

RECESS RULES!

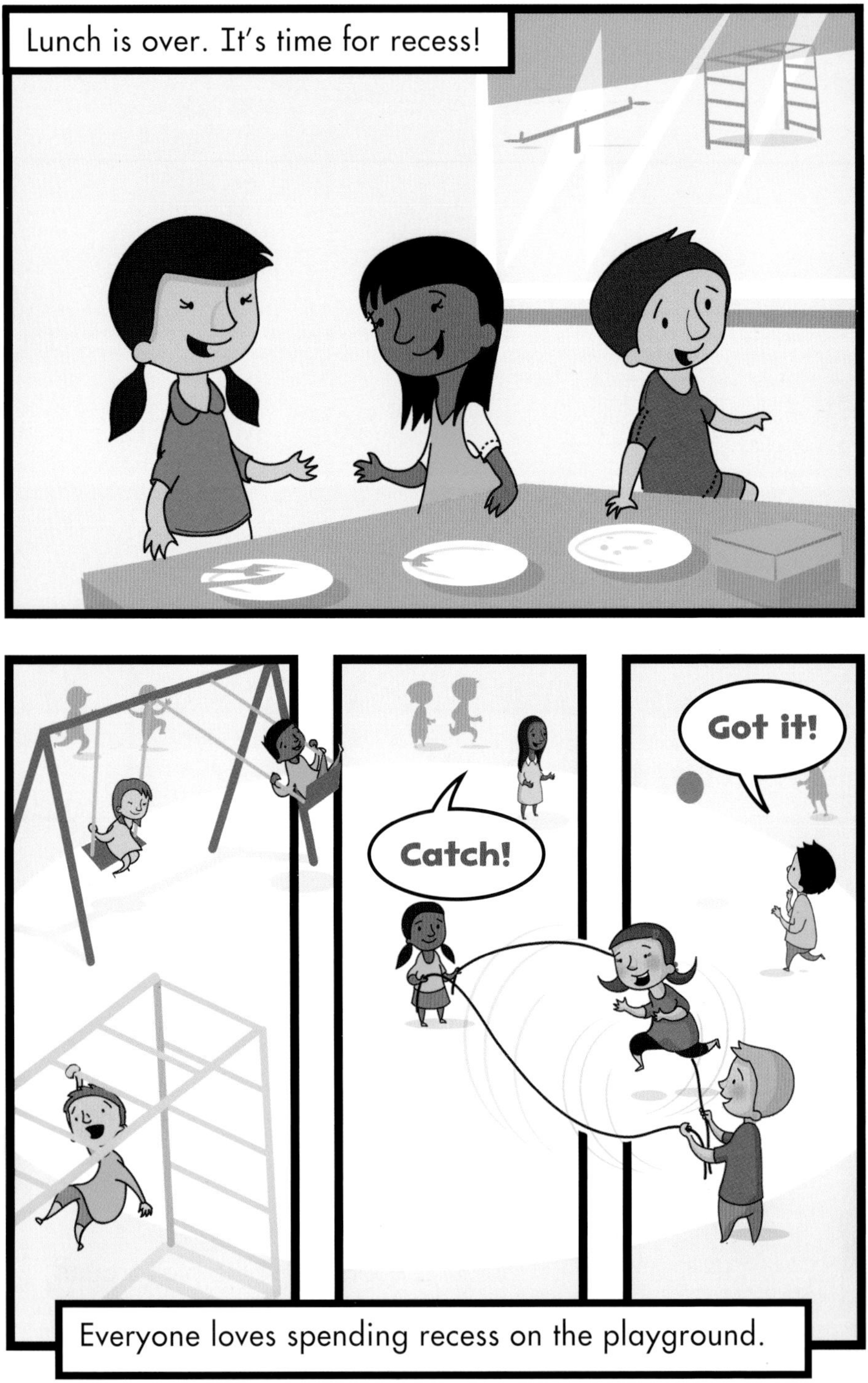
Lunch is over. It's time for recess!
Catch!
Got it!
Everyone loves spending recess on the playground.

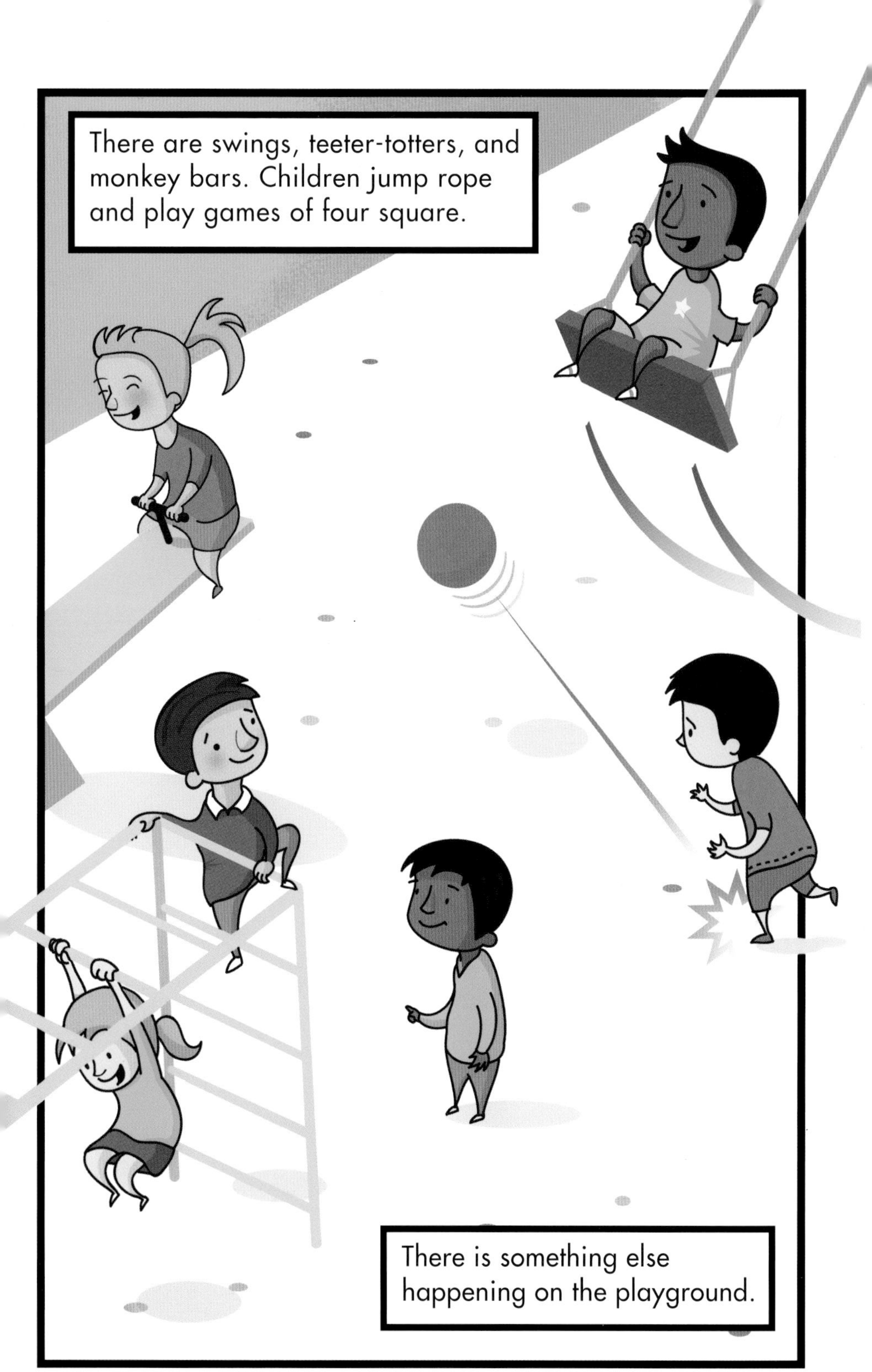
There are swings, teeter-totters, and monkey bars. Children jump rope and play games of four square.
There is something else happening on the playground.

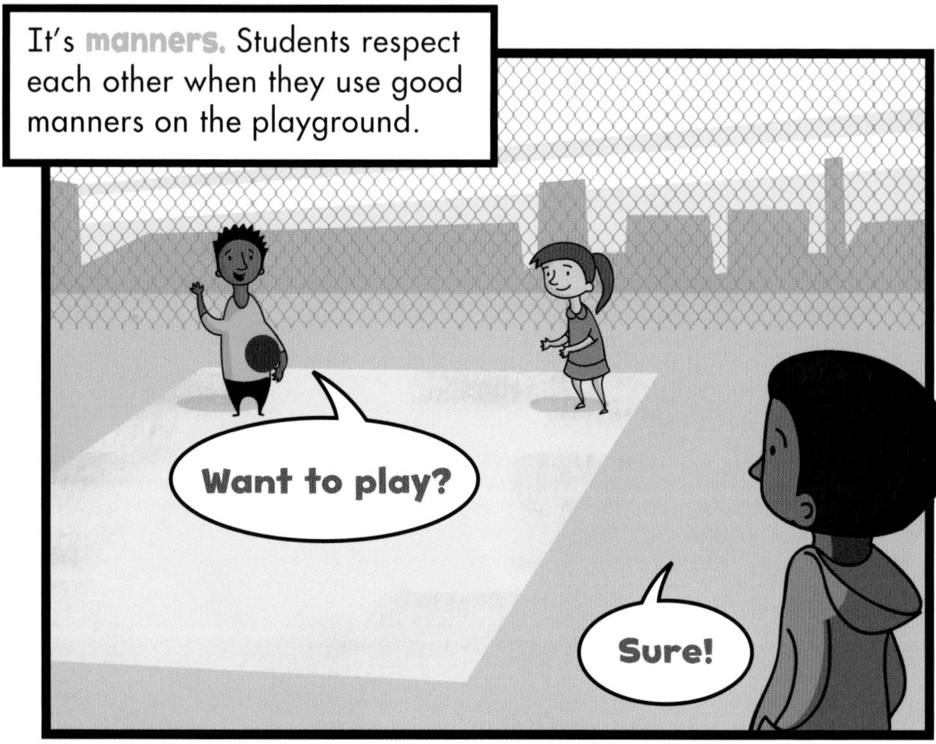
It's manners. Students respect each other when they use good manners on the playground.
Want to play?
Sure!

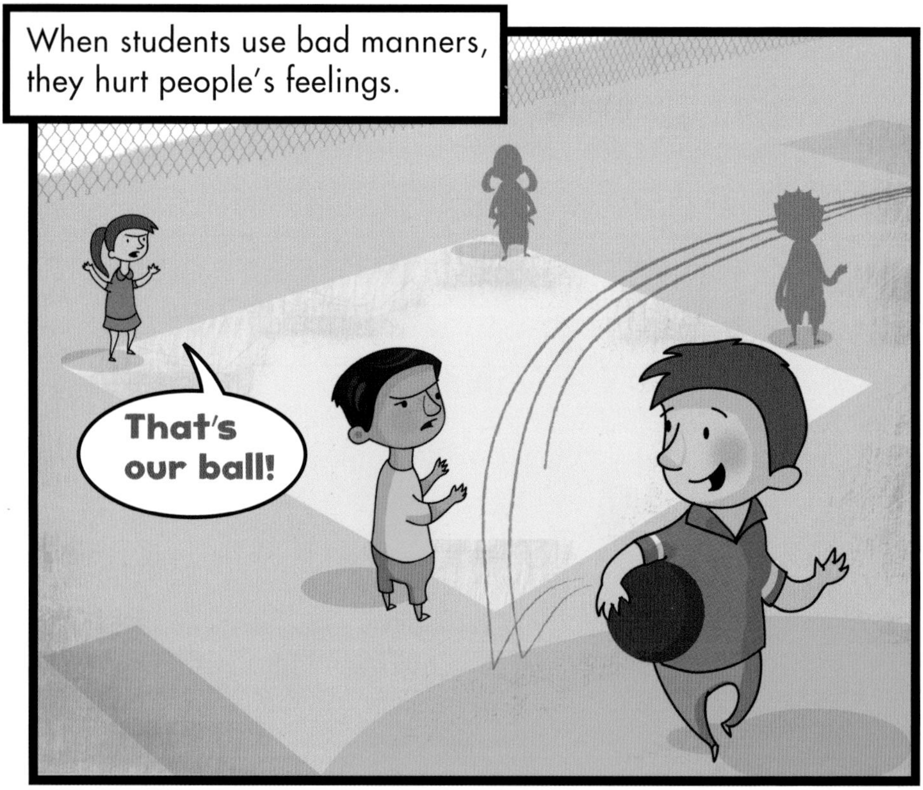
When students use bad manners, they hurt people's feelings.
That's our ball!

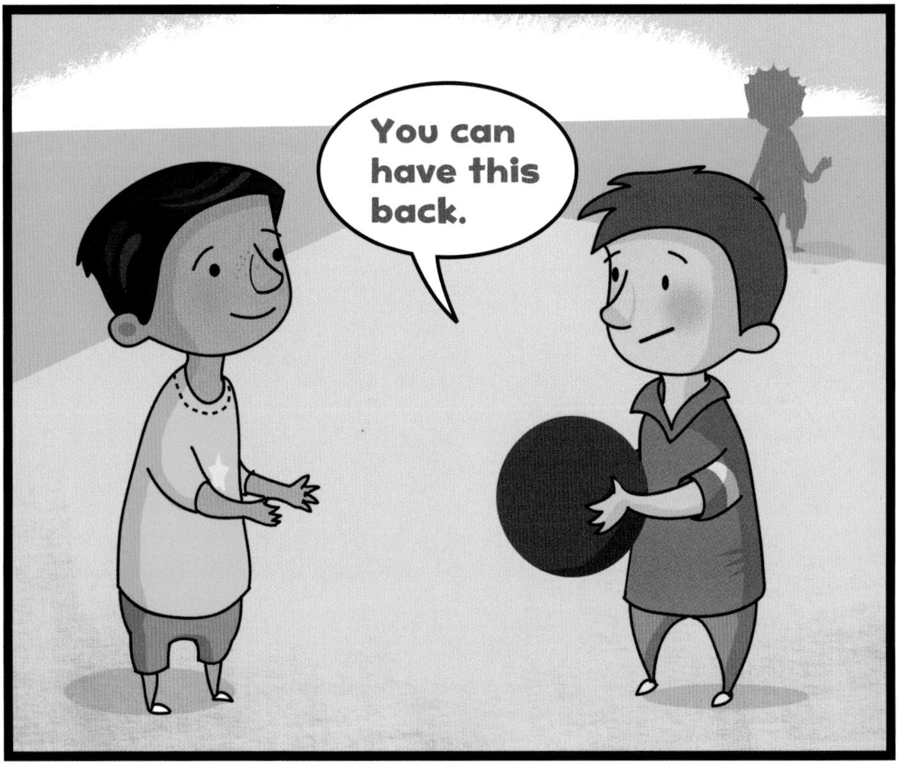
You can have this back.

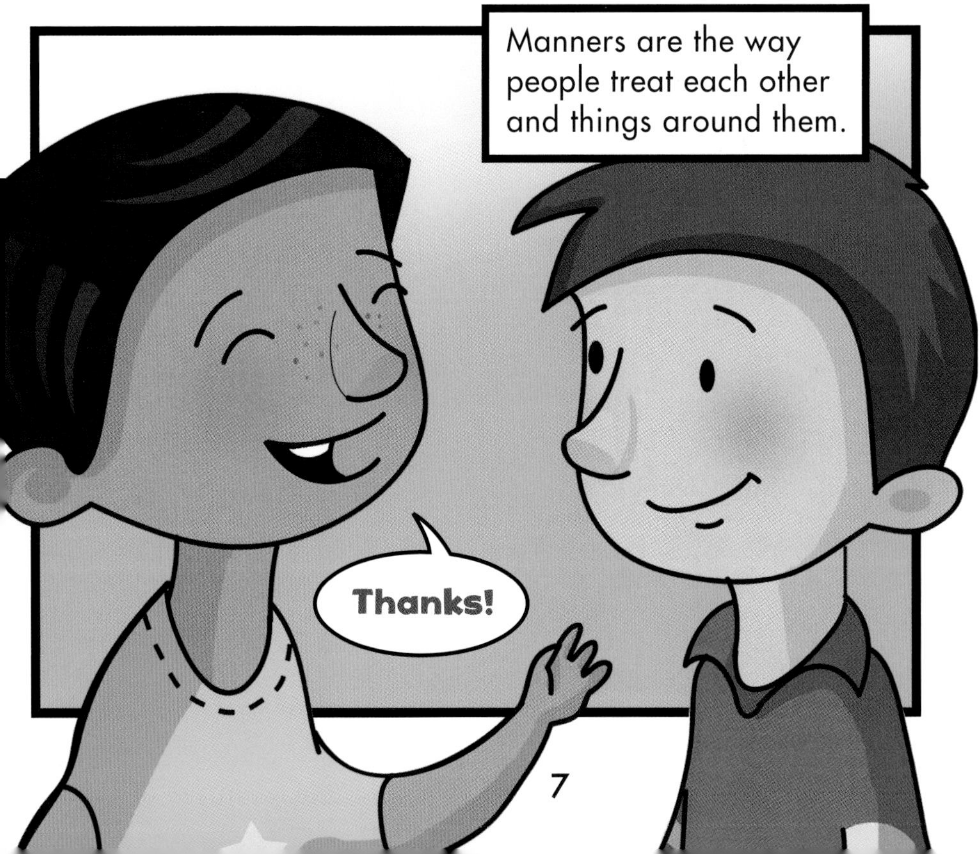
Manners are the way people treat each other and things around them.
Thanks!

Look Around

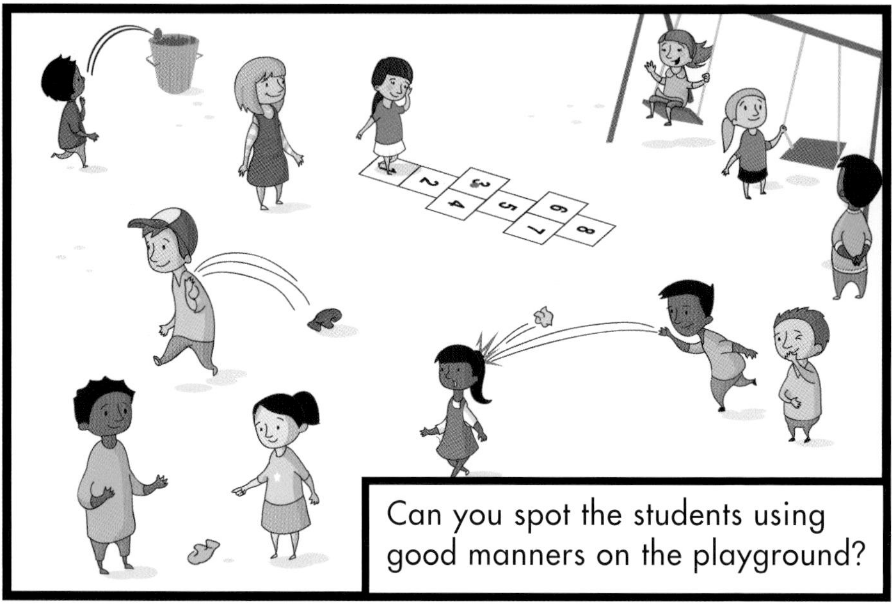
Can you spot the students using good manners on the playground?

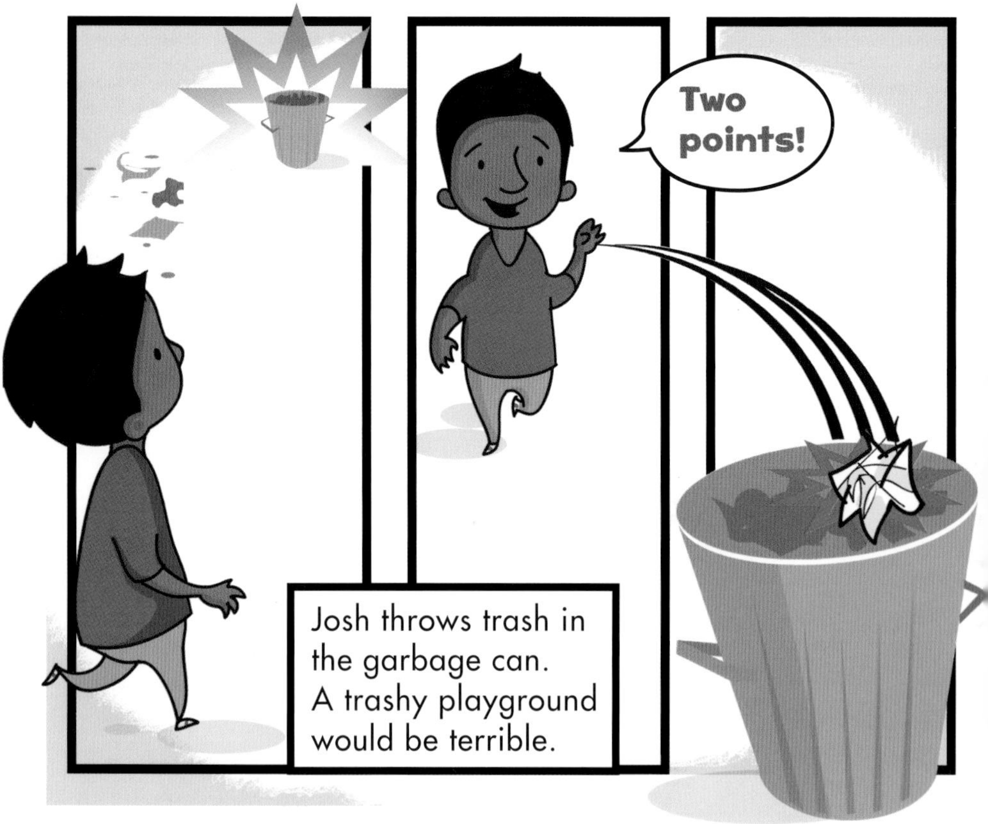
Two points!
Josh throws trash in the garbage can. A trashy playground would be terrible.

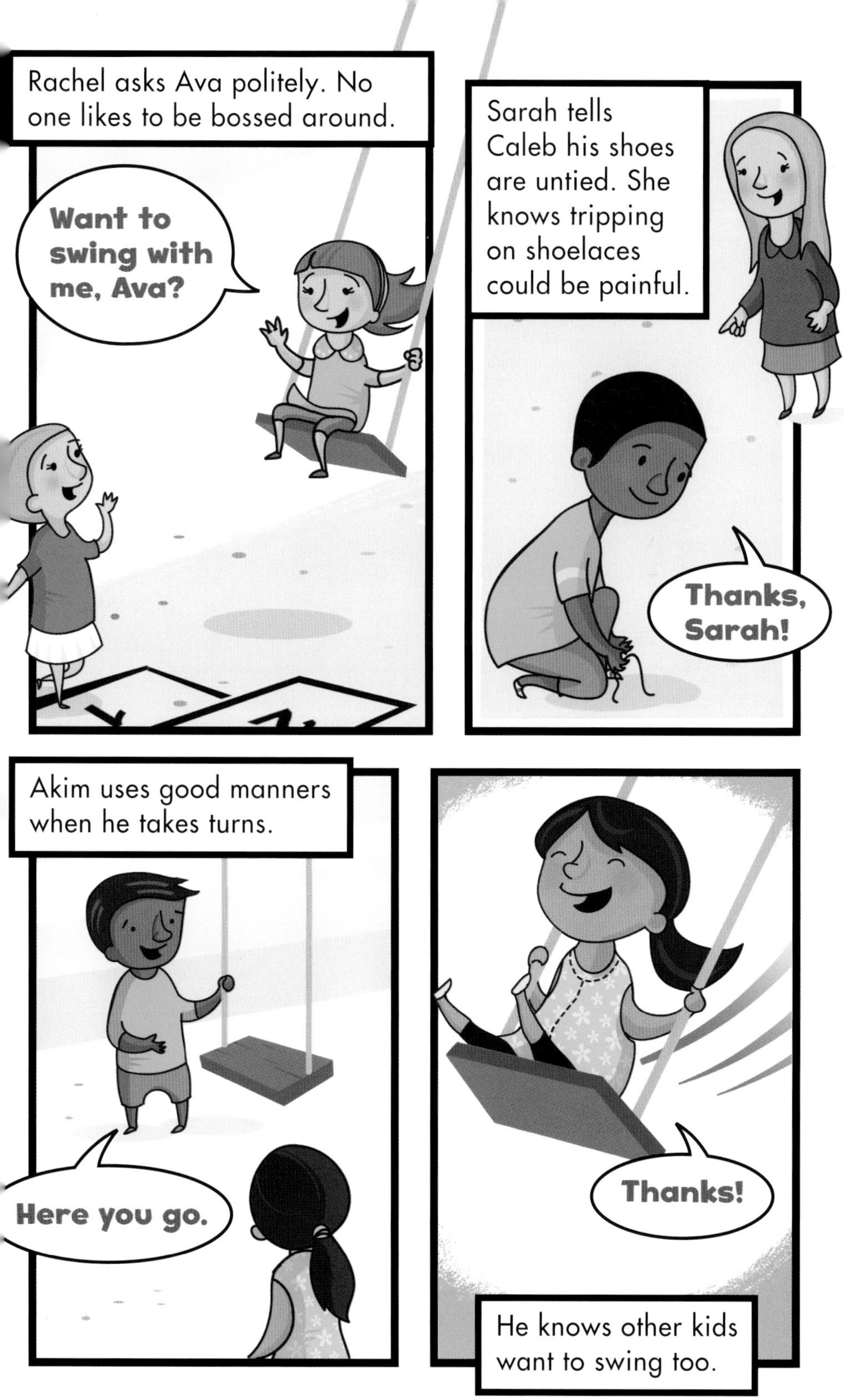
Rachel asks Ava politely. No one likes to be bossed around.
Want to swing with me, Ava?
Sarah tells Caleb his shoes are untied. She knows tripping on shoelaces could be painful.
Thanks, Sarah!
Akim uses good manners when he takes turns.
Here you go.
Thanks!
He knows other kids want to swing too.

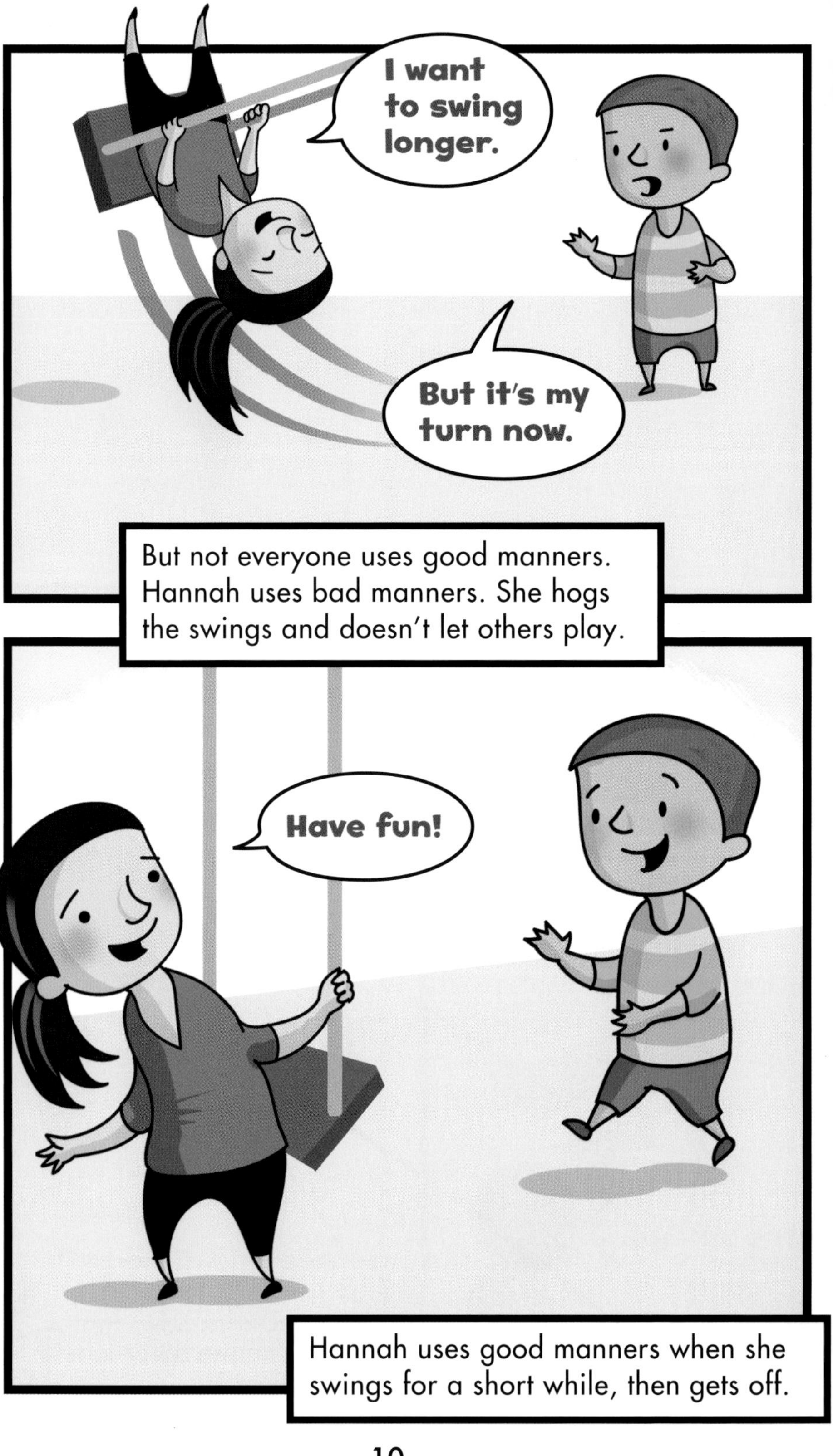
I want to swing longer.
But it's my turn now.
But not everyone uses good manners. Hannah uses bad manners. She hogs the swings and doesn't let others play.
Have fun!
Hannah uses good manners when she swings for a short while, then gets off.

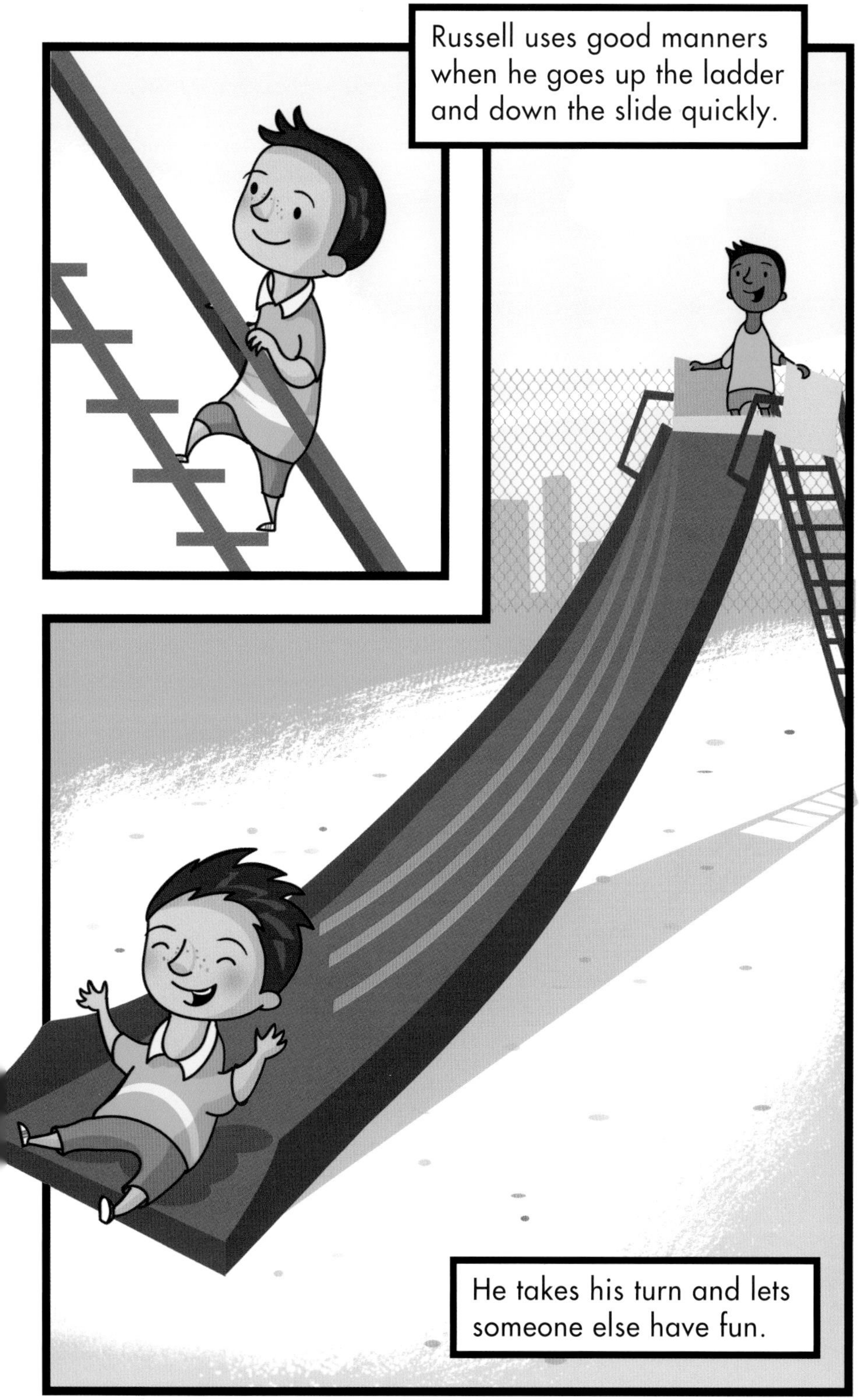
Russell uses good manners when he goes up the ladder and down the slide quickly.
He takes his turn and lets someone else have fun.

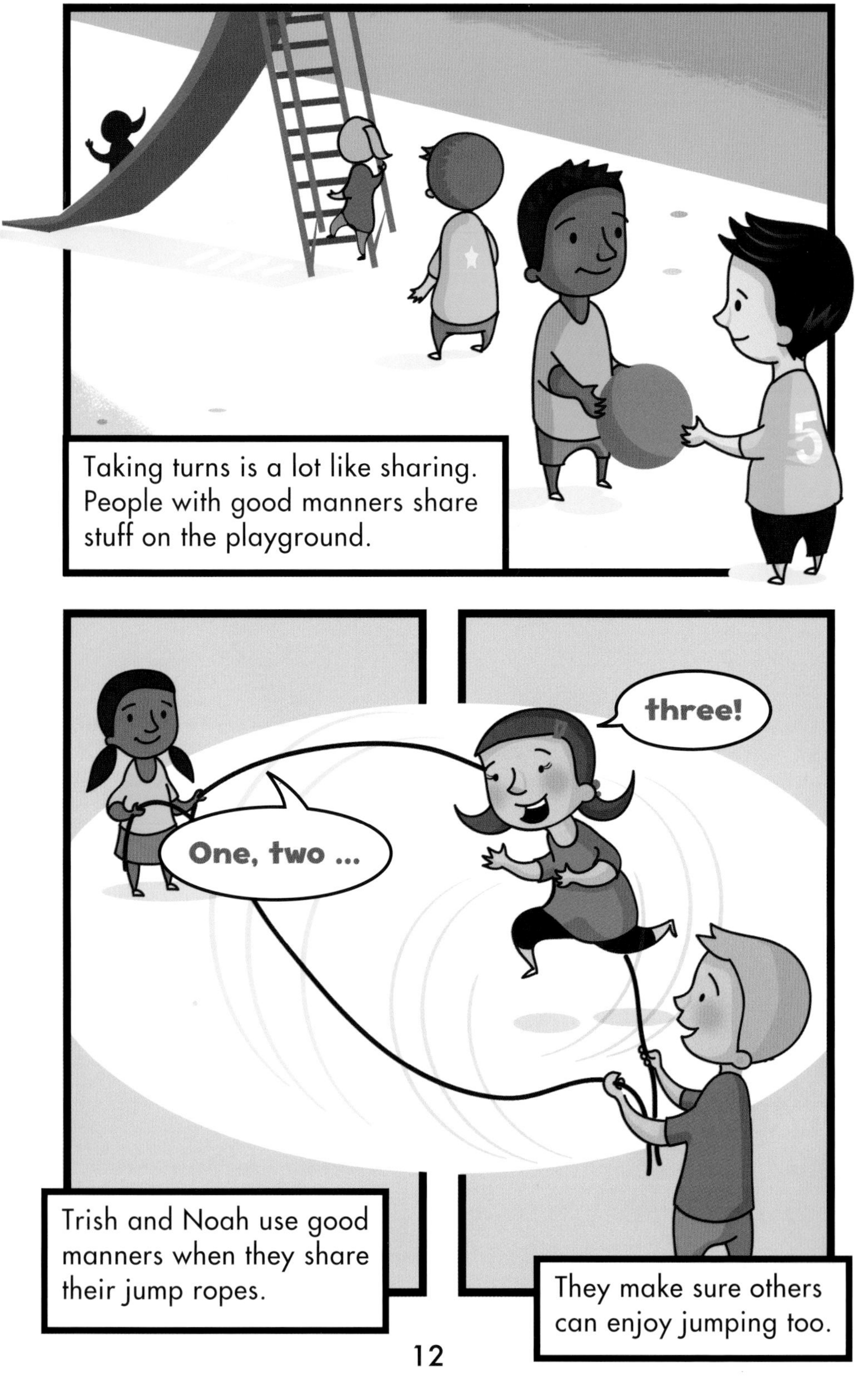
Taking turns is a lot like sharing. People with good manners share stuff on the playground.
5
Trish and Noah use good manners when they share their jump ropes.
One, two ...
three!
They make sure others can enjoy jumping too.

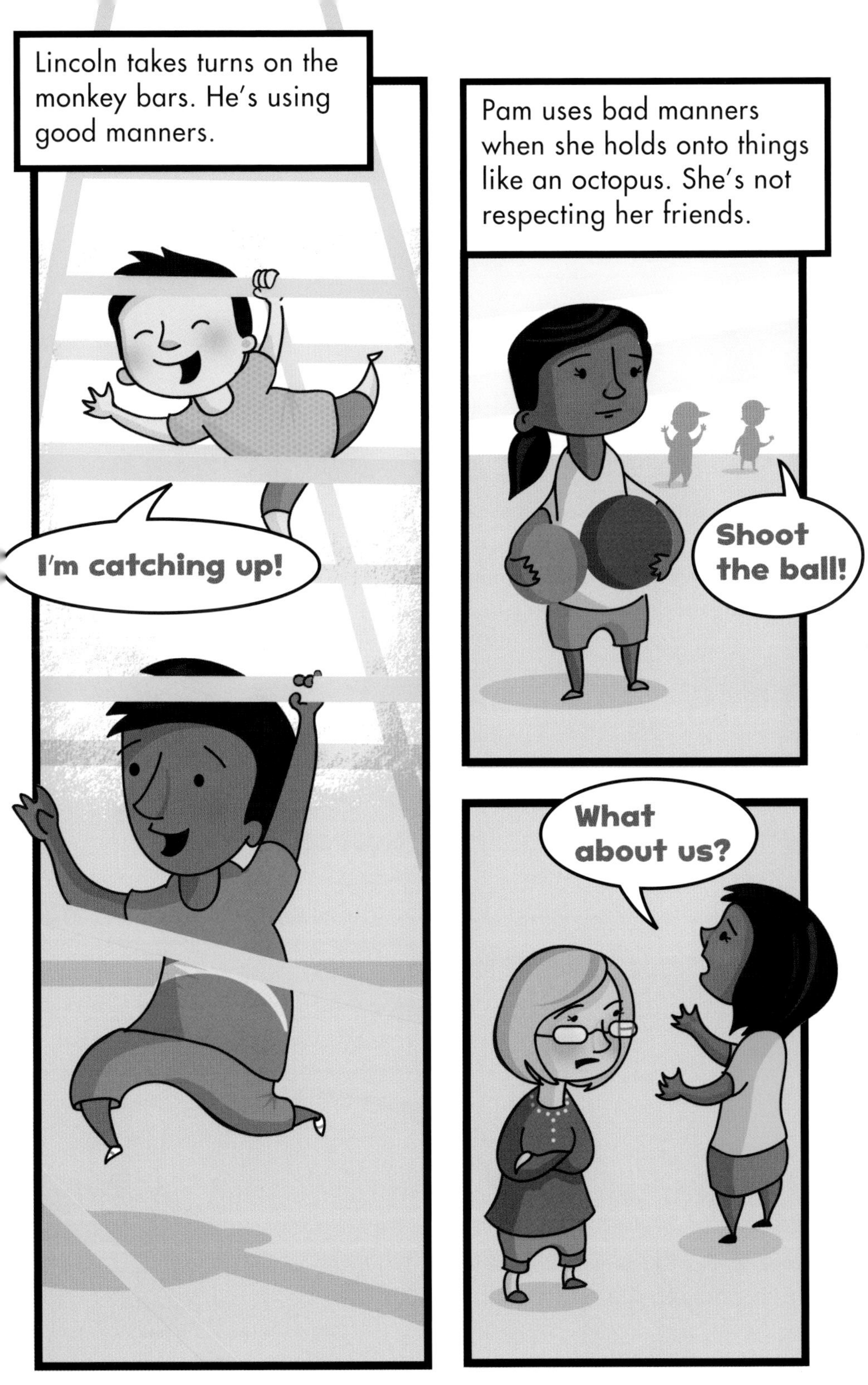
Lincoln takes turns on the monkey bars. He's using good manners.
I'm catching up!
Pam uses bad manners when she holds onto things like an octopus. She's not respecting her friends.
Shoot the ball!
What about us?

What Do You Say?

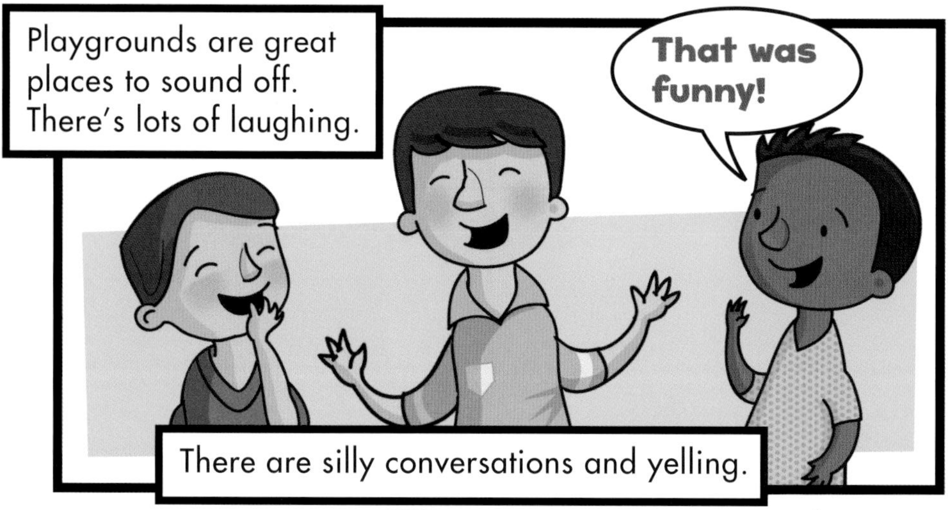
Playgrounds are great places to sound off. There's lots of laughing.
That was funny!
There are silly conversations and yelling.

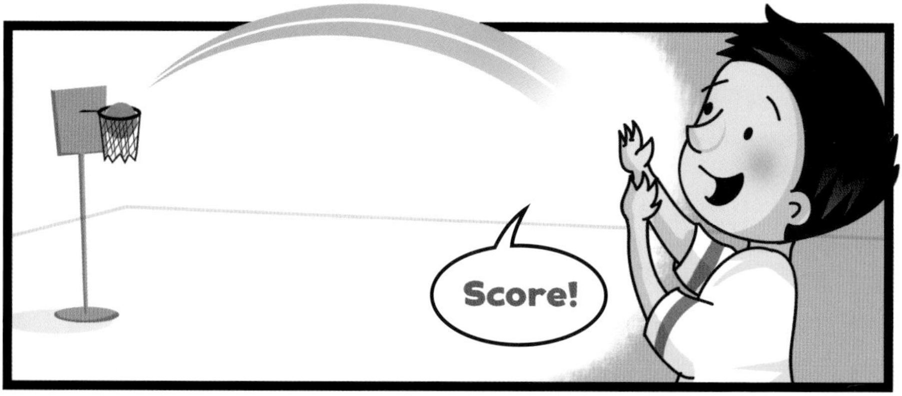
Score!

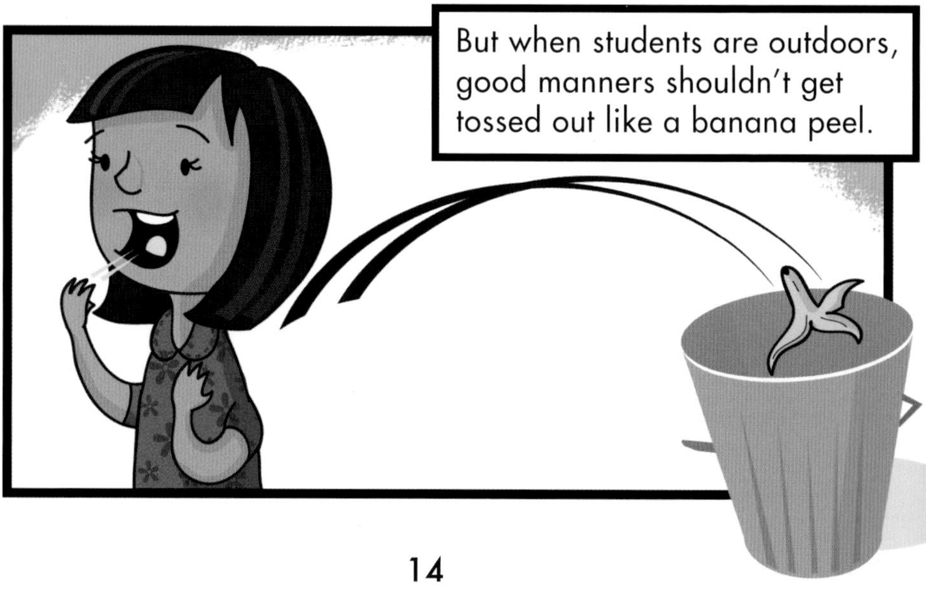
But when students are outdoors, good manners shouldn't get tossed out like a banana peel.

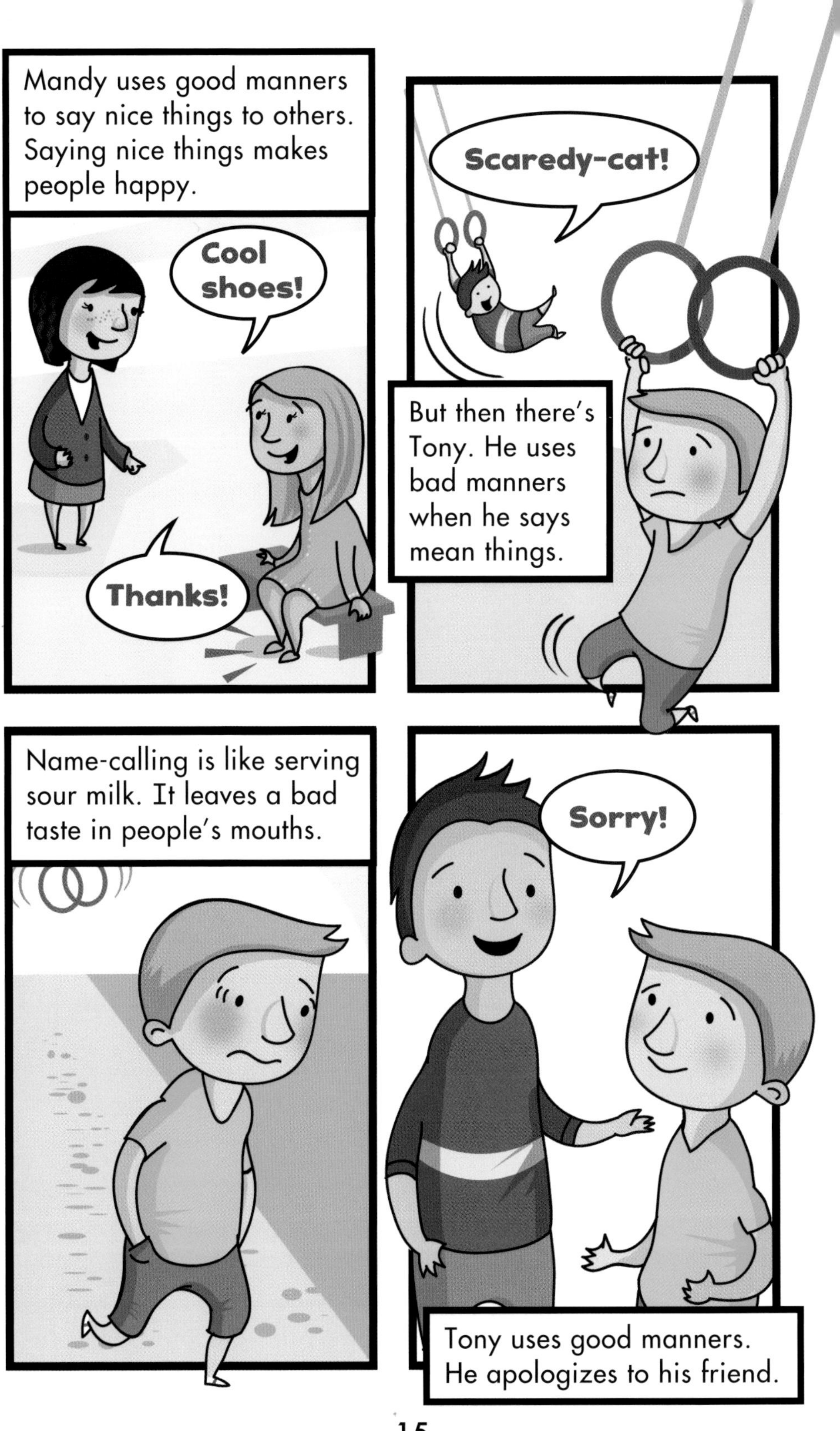

Mandy uses good manners to say nice things to others. Saying nice things makes people happy.
Cool shoes!
Thanks!
Scaredy-cat!
But then there's Tony. He uses bad manners when he says mean things.
Name-calling is like serving sour milk. It leaves a bad taste in people's mouths.
Sorry!
Tony uses good manners. He apologizes to his friend.

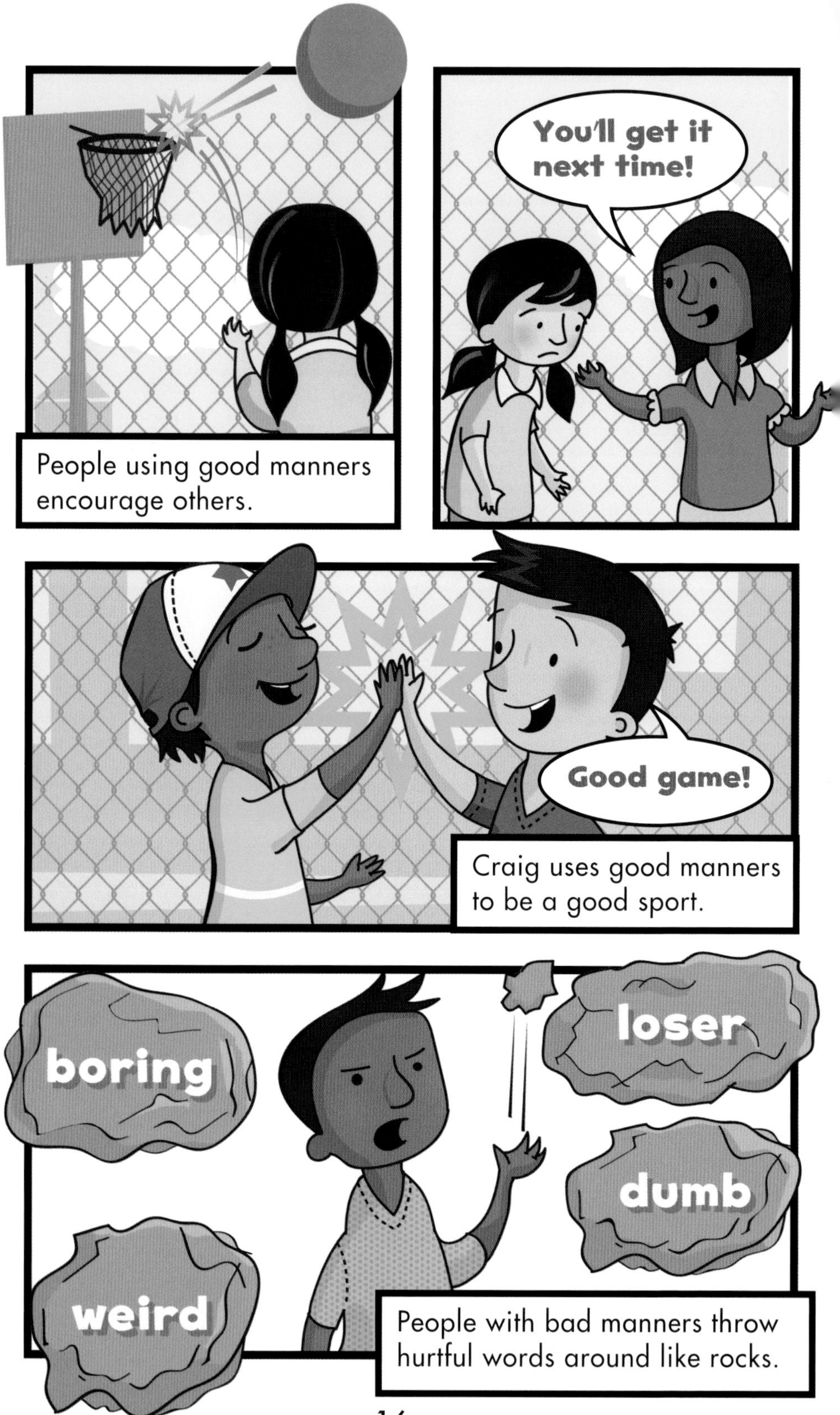
People using good manners encourage others.
You'll get it next time!
Good game!
Craig uses good manners to be a good sport.
boring
loser
dumb
weird
People with bad manners throw hurtful words around like rocks.

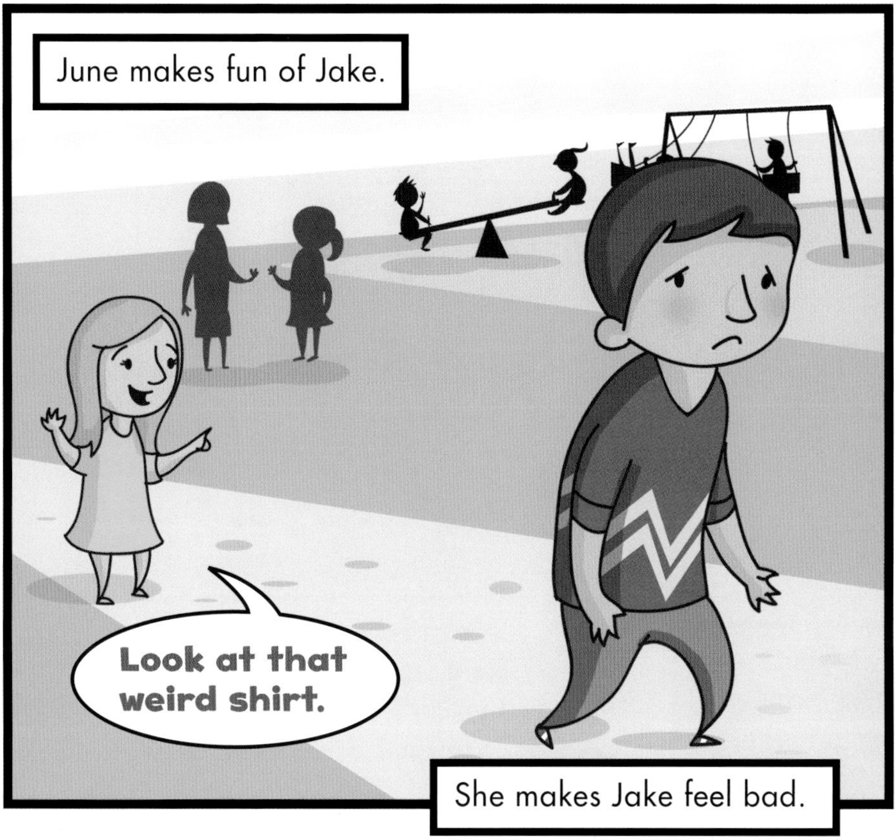
June makes fun of Jake.
Look at that weird shirt.
She makes Jake feel bad.

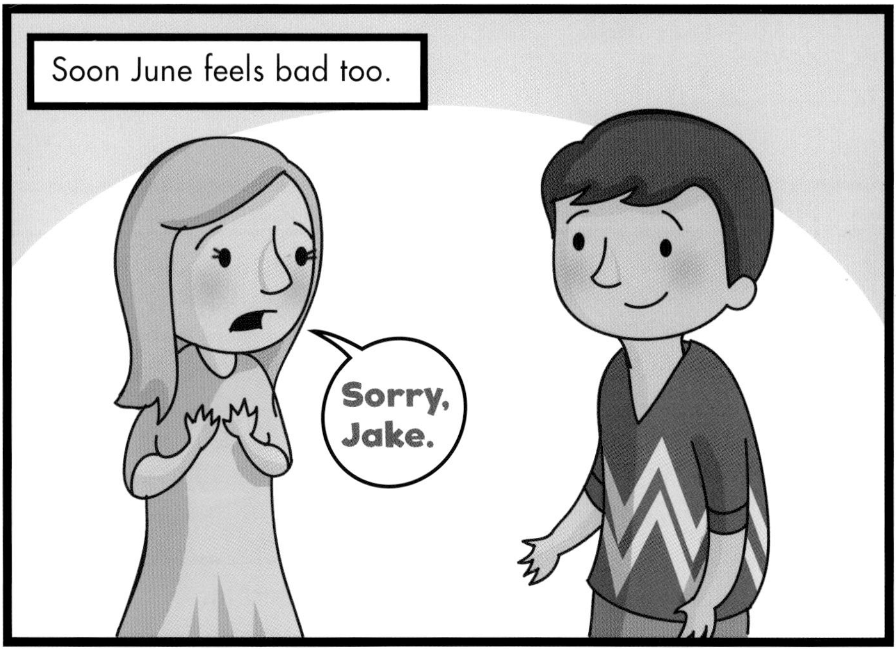
Soon June feels bad too.
Sorry, Jake.

PLAYING AROUND

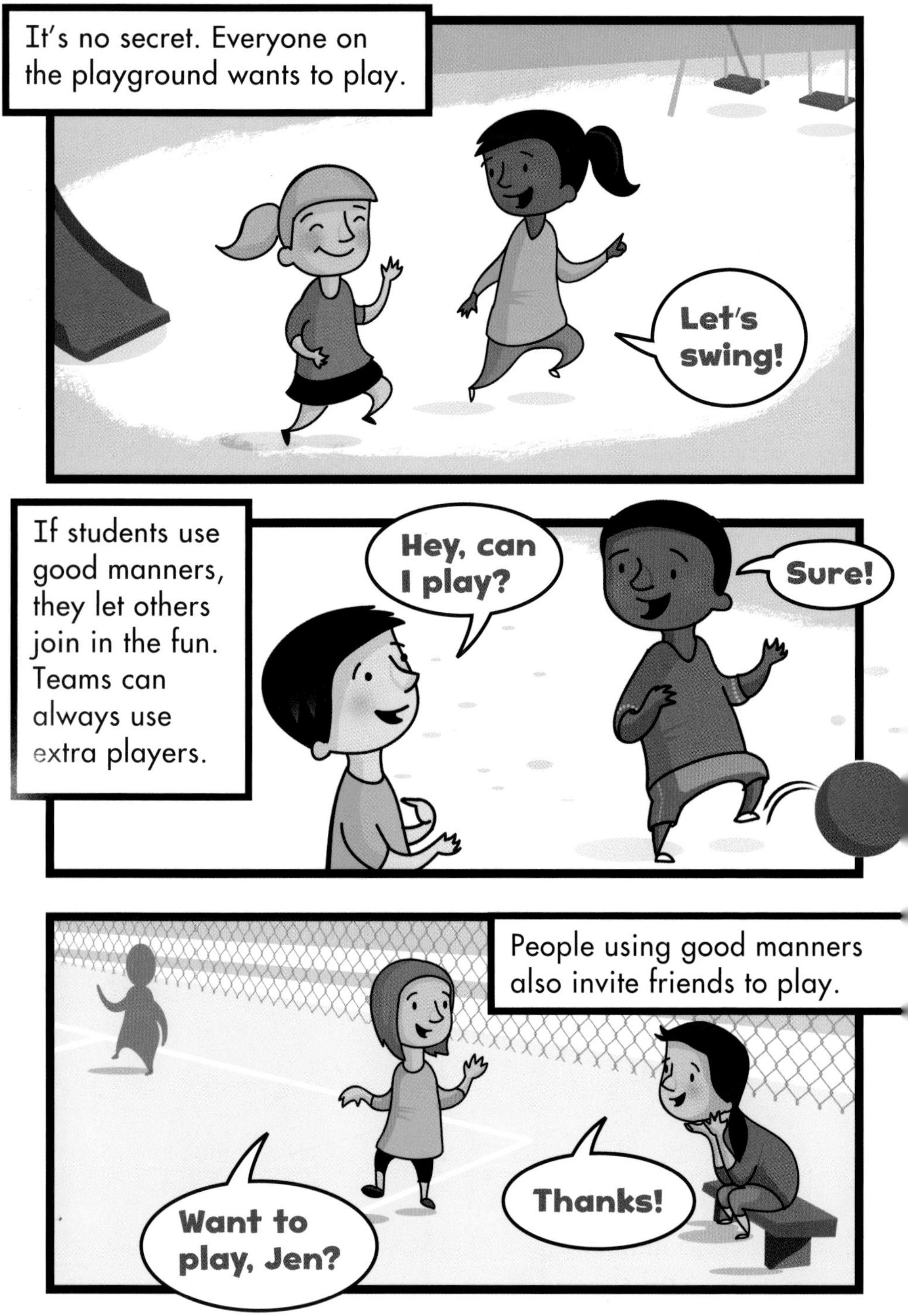
It's no secret. Everyone on the playground wants to play.
Let's swing!
If students use good manners, they let others join in the fun. Teams can always use extra players.
Hey, can I play?
Sure!
People using good manners also invite friends to play.
Want to play, Jen?
Thanks!

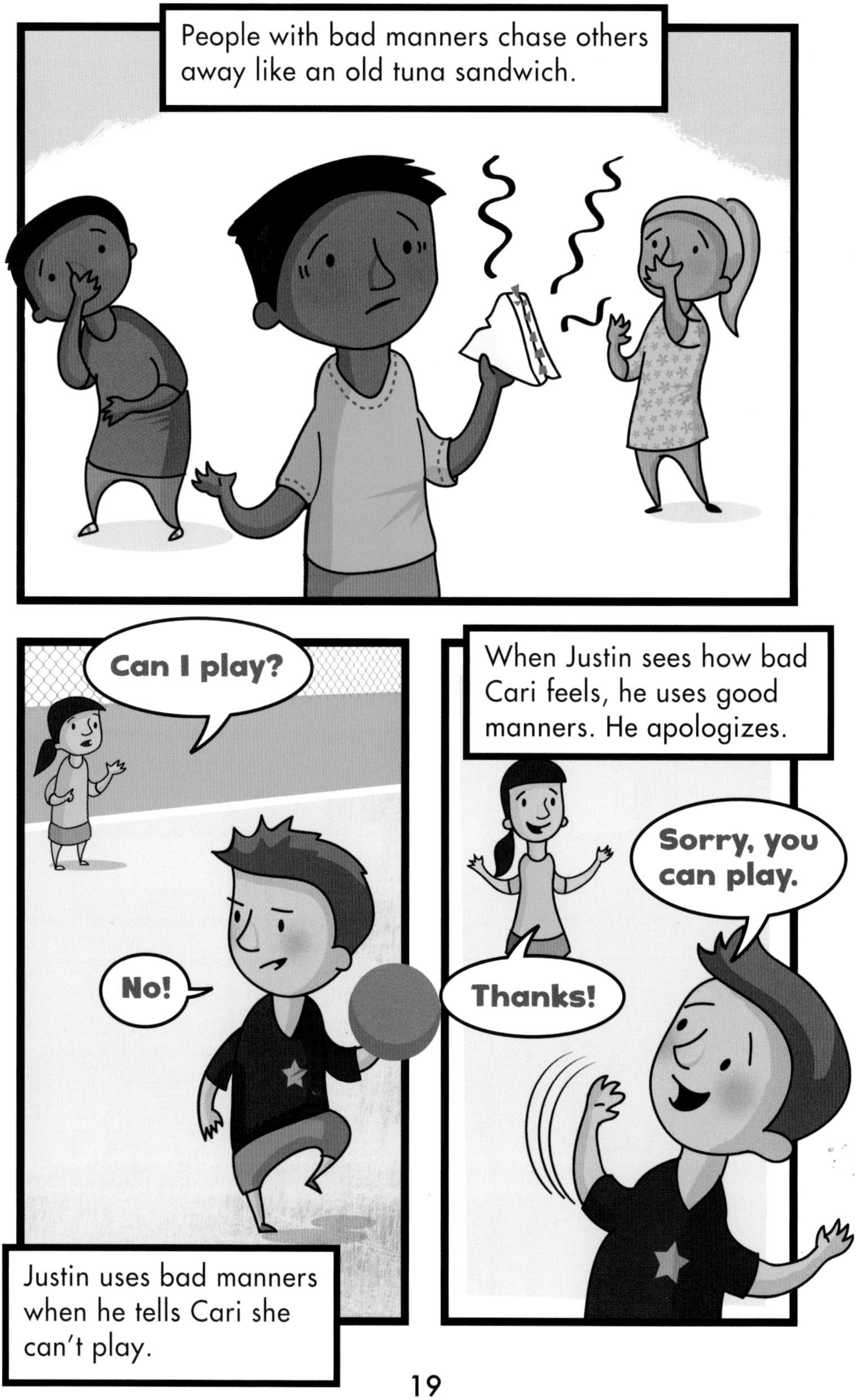
People with bad manners chase others away like an old tuna sandwich.
Can I play?
No!
Justin uses bad manners when he tells Cari she can't play.
When Justin sees how bad Cari feels, he uses good manners. He apologizes.
Sorry, you can play.
Thanks!

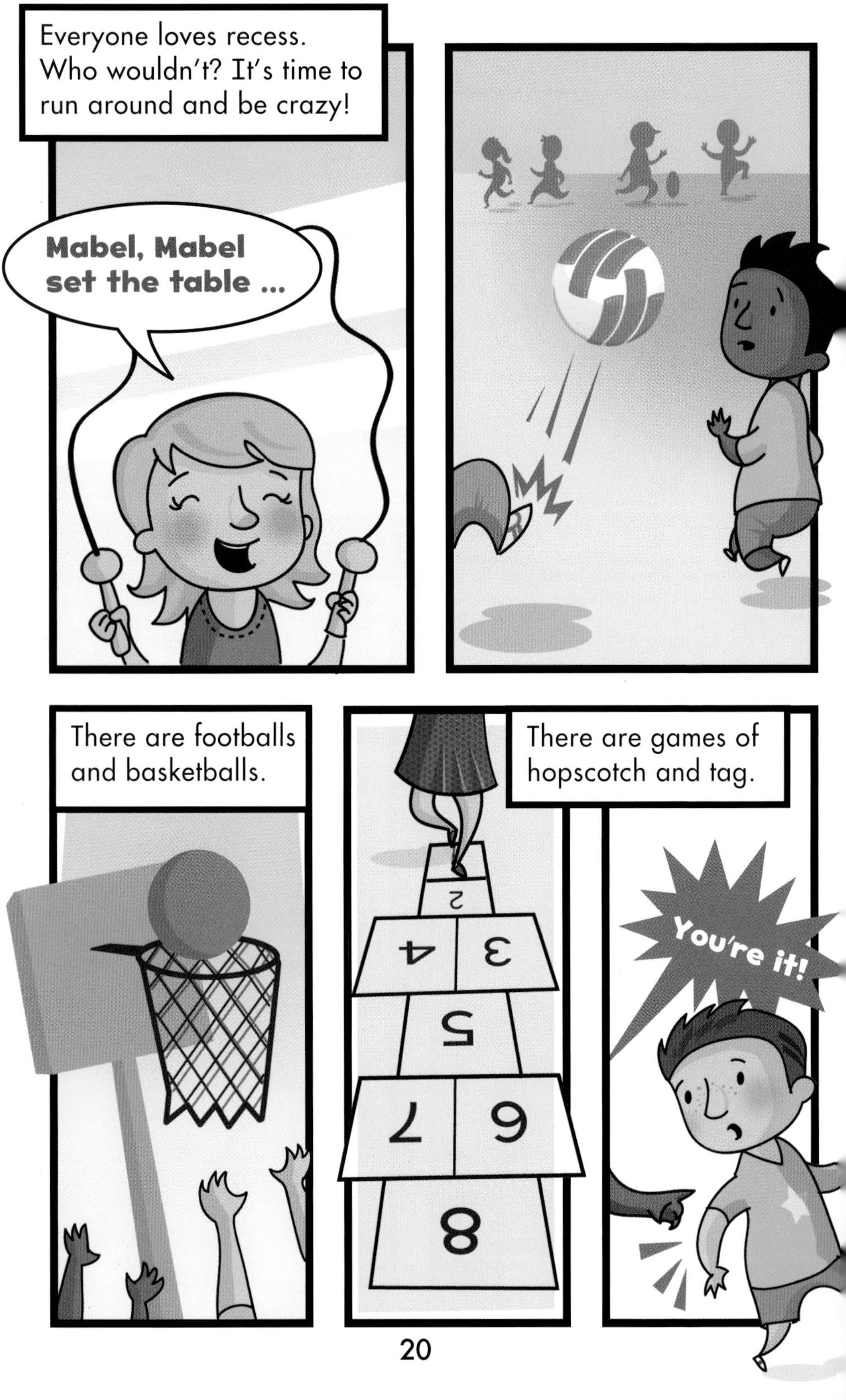

Everyone loves recess. Who wouldn't? It's time to run around and be crazy!
Mabel, Mabel set the table ...
There are footballs and basketballs.
There are games of hopscotch and tag.
You're it!

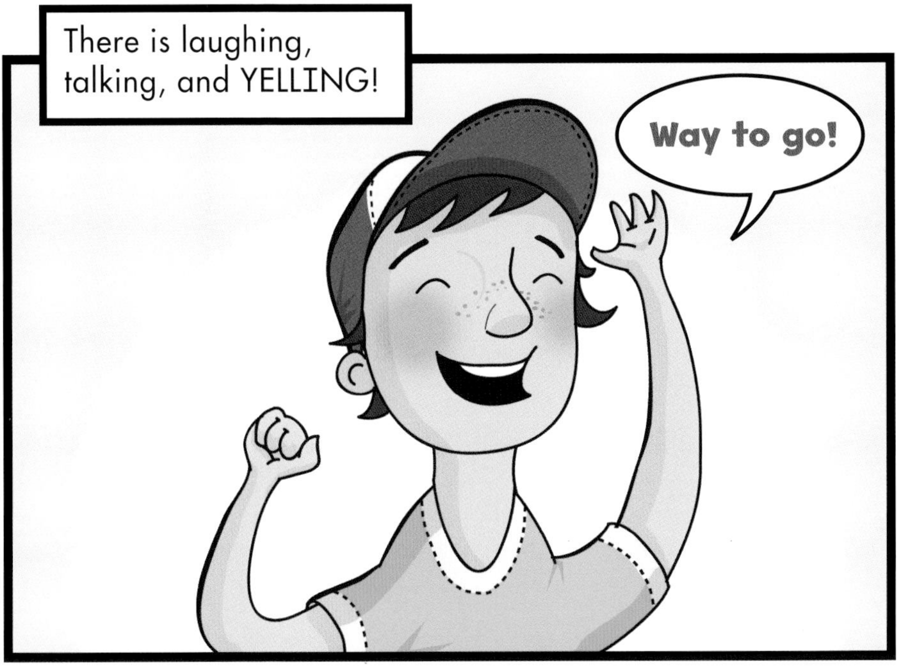
There is laughing, talking, and YELLING!
Way to go!

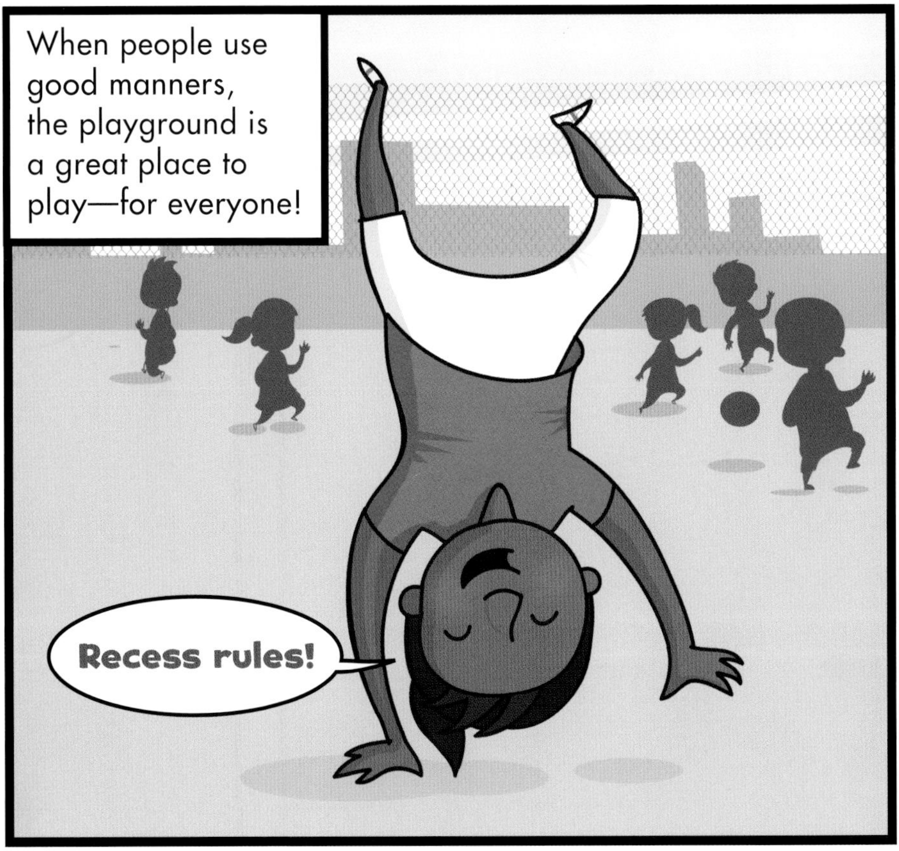
When people use good manners, the playground is a great place to play—for everyone!
Recess rules!

GLOSSARY

apologize—to say sorry

conversation—spoken words between two or more people

encourage—to give praise and support to someone

respect—to show you care; respect means to treat others the way you would like to be treated

22

READ MORE

Finn, Carrie. *Manners at School.* Way to Be! Minneapolis: Picture Window Books, 2007.

Keller, Laurie. *Do Unto Otters: A Book about Manners.* New York: Henry Holt, 2007.

Sierra, Judy. *Mind Your Manners, B. B. Wolf.* New York: Knopf, 2007.

Tourville, Amanda Doering. *Manners on the School Bus.* Way to Be! Minneapolis: Picture Window Books, 2009.

INTERNET SITES

FactHound offers a safe, fun way to find Internet sites related to this book. All of the sites on FactHound have been researched by our staff.

Here's all you do:

Visit *www.facthound.com*

Type in this code: 9781429653329

Super-cool stuff!

Check out projects, games and lots more at
www.capstonekids.com

INDEX

FIRST GRAPHICS

Manners Matter

TITLES IN THIS SET:

MANNERS MATTER IN THE CLASSROOM

MANNERS MATTER IN THE LIBRARY

MANNERS MATTER ON A FIELD TRIP

MANNERS MATTER ON THE PLAYGROUND